Tongues: To Speak or
Not To Speak

Tongues: To Speak or Not To Speak

by

DONALD W. BURDICK

MOODY PRESS

CHICAGO

Library of Congress Catalog Card Number: 76-80940

Second Printing, 1970

Third Printing, 1971

Fifth Printing, 1972

Sixth Printing, 1972

Seventh Printing, 1973

ISBN: 0-8024-8795-5

Printed in the United States of America

Contents

Introduction

// 'yamana 'kita ,sia'naya,si // 'yamana 'kita ,sia'-
naya,si // ,ana'kiana 'tiasa,naya ,ana'kia 'tana 'sia,-
naya,si //

African language, Philippine dialect, or the speech
of angels—which is it? The linguist who transcribed
this glossolalic speech could not identify it.[1] Whatever
it is, however, this sample of tongues speaking is not
unlike that which is practiced by sincere Christians of
various denominations in many places around the
world today.

On New Year's Eve, 1900, at the Bethel Bible College of Topeka, Kansas, a student named Agnes Ozman
asked the director of the school to lay his hands on
her head and pray that she might receive the baptism
of the Holy Spirit. When he did so, immediately Miss
Ozman spoke fluently in syllables which no one understood. This occurrence was the beginning of the modern
Pentecostal movement.[2] From Topeka by way of Hou-
ston, Texas, the tongues phenomenon spread to Los
Angeles, where it resulted in the Azusa Mission, which
was destined to be the center of Pentecostalism for a
number of years.

[1]Walter A. Wolfram, "The Sociolinguistics of Glossolalia" (unpublished Master's thesis), p. 97.
[2]John L. Sherrill, *They Speak with Other Tongues*, p. 38.

From these unpretentious beginnings sprang the great variety of present-day Pentecostal groups, including such churches as the Assemblies of God, the United Pentecostal Church and the Church of God. Through the years Pentecostal congregations have experienced phenomenal growth, thriving especially on the failure of the old-line denominations to foster a vital, experiential Christianity. Many of the Pentecostal churches have steadily climbed the socioeconomic ladder with the result that they are now appealing to the solid middle-class type of person.

For the most part the Pentecostal viewpoint was confined to Pentecostal churches until the late 1950's and early 60's when, as John Sherrill puts it, "The walls came tumbling down." It began to be apparent that more and more people in the traditional churches were speaking in tongues. The event which focused national attention on this new invasion occurred on April 3, 1960, at the 2,600-member St. Mark's Episcopal Church in Van Nuys, California. Father Dennis Bennett, the rector of this influential church, received the gift of tongues and upon announcing the fact was forced to resign. The news media, including *Time* and *Newsweek*, reported the story across the country.[3]

Now that "the cat was out of the bag" reports of other old-line church leaders who had received the gift of tongues began to be heard. They included William Nelson, editor of the American Baptist Convention publication *Frontier;* Frank Downing, Southern Baptist pastor of Baltimore, Maryland; Harald Bredesen, pastor of the First Reformed Church, Mount Vernon, New York; Larry Christenson, pastor of Trinity Lutheran Church, San Pedro, California; and numerous

[3]*Ibid.,* pp. 61-62. Cf. Morton T. Kelsey, *Tongue Speaking: An Experiment in Spiritual Experience,* pp. 98-102.

others of various denominations in all parts of the country. These were not people from Pentecostal congregations in the lower economic strata; they were leaders of staid middle- or upper-class traditional churches, some of which were highly liturgical.

Obviously strange forces were at work producing most unexpected results. What does it take to move an Episcopalian rector to accept a central distinctive of Pentecostalism? What is this experience which is able to penetrate the defenses of a formal Lutheran pastor? How can the spread of neo-Pentecostalism be explained? Is it a renewal of the New Testament phenomenon of glossolalia? And if not, what is this strangely baffling but undeniable experience?

GENUINE BIBLICAL
GLOSSOLALIA

1

The Nature of Glossolalia

In order to find the answers to questions which neo-Pentecostalism creates, we must analyze the phenomenon of glossolalia as it appears in the New Testament. The term "glossolalia" is an Anglicized compound made up of two Greek words: *glōssa* ("tongue") and *lalia* ("speech"). It therefore means tongue-speech or speaking in tongues.

It is our purpose in this section to discover what the Bible teaches concerning genuine glossolalia, its nature, its purpose and its duration.

The places where tongues are explicitly referred to in the Bible are few in number. It is noteworthy that Jesus is never said to have spoken in tongues even though the Spirit came upon Him at His baptism, an experience which Peter described as an anointing "with the Holy Ghost and with power" (Acts 10:38). And John declares that "God giveth not the Spirit by measure unto him" (John 3:34).[1] Although Christ received the Spirit without limitation, there is no evidence that He ever spoke in tongues.

[1]Although the Greek text does not contain the words "unto him," both the context of the statement and an understanding of human finitude make it evident that John is speaking of Christ as recipient of the Spirit. It cannot be said that any mere finite man could receive the infinite Spirit of God without limit. Such an experience would be beyond human capacity. This could only be true of One who is Deity.

The one passage in the Gospels which explicitly speaks of tongues is Mark 16:17-18:

> And these signs shall follow them that believe; In my name they shall cast out devils; they shall speak with new tongues; they shall take up serpents; and if any drink any deadly thing, it shall not hurt them; they shall lay hands on the sick, and they shall recover.

This passage, however, is not solid ground on which to build any doctrine, inasmuch as textual scholars are agreed that Mark 16:9-20 was not a part of the original Marcan text. The most trustworthy extant Greek manuscripts end with Mark 16:8. Thus, as far as the record goes, Jesus neither practiced glossolalia nor did He explicitly mention the subject.

There are numerous other passages in the New Testament which are interpreted as referring to tongues, such as Ephesians 5:18-19:

> And be not drunk with wine, wherein is excess; but be filled with the Spirit; speaking to yourselves in psalms and hymns and spiritual songs, singing and making melody in your heart to the Lord.

These verses, however, contain no explicit mention of tongues, and it is debatable whether Paul had this experience in mind when he penned them. Statements such as this cannot be used to provide a basis for a valid doctrine of tongues.

Consequently, we are left with but four passages where explicit references to tongues are to be found. They are:

Acts 2:1-13—tongues on the day of Pentecost
Acts 10:44-47; 11:15-18—tongues at the house of Cornelius

Acts 19:1-7—tongues and John's disciples

I Corinthians 12:1—14:40—misuse of tongues at Corinth

In Acts the references are in the nature of historical accounts; in I Corinthians they are doctrinal, written with the intention of correcting the misuse of the gift by some in the church.

Tongues on the Day of Pentecost (Acts 2:1-13)

This passage recounts the earliest appearance of tongues as a Christian phenomenon. In verse 4 Luke says: "And they were all filled with the Holy Ghost, and began to speak with other tongues, as the Spirit gave them utterance." The term "tongue" (*glōssa*) was commonly used in Greek to refer both to the physical organ of speech (Luke 1:64) and to the speech or language which the physical organ produces. Here the word "other" (*heterais*) suggests that the believers spoke in different languages from that which was native to them, a fact which is borne out by the surprise described in verses 7-8. This is further confirmed by verse 6, where it is said that "every man heard them speak in his own language." The word translated as "language" is *dialektō* from which our word "dialect" comes. The two terms "tongue" (*glōssa*) and "language" (*dialektos*) are obviously used interchangeably here, making it clear that the disciples were speaking in other languages. What those languages were is indicated in verses 8-11, namely, the native languages of such areas as Parthia, Media, Elam, Mesopotamia, Judea, Cappadocia, Pontus, Asia and Phrygia.

There can, therefore, be no doubt that the tongues described in Acts 2 were foreign languages. The phenomenon was a miracle enabling the disciples to speak

in languages which were not native to them and which
they had not learned by normal educative processes.

A comparison with the other passages which mention glossolalia will show that the clearest description
of the nature of tongues is that found in Acts 2. In no
other place is there an explicit statement as to the real
nature of tongues-speech. Here we see glossolalia in its
unperverted form as God intended it, not as it later
came to be misused in the Corinthian church. We are
therefore justified in viewing the account in Acts 2 as
the definitive description of what New Testament
tongues really were.

On this basis we may regard the Acts passage as
establishing the guidelines for all later and less obvious
references to tongues. We will, then, understand
tongues in all succeeding accounts as being the miracle
of speaking foreign languages which had not previously
been learned. In the examination of the remaining
passages, we will seek to ascertain whether or not they
bear out this assumption.

Tongues at the House of Cornelius (Acts 10:44-47; 11:15-18)

When Peter, under divine duress, took the gospel
message to the Gentiles gathered at the house of Cornelius, "the Holy Ghost fell on all them which heard
the word," and they spoke with tongues (Acts 10:44,
46). Although the account does not specifically say
that these tongues were foreign languages, it implies as
much. The Jewish believers were amazed that God
also had given the Spirit to the Gentiles (v. 45), which
suggests that the latter had received the same experience as the Jews had previously been given. Also Peter
and his companions said that the Gentiles had "received
the Holy Ghost as well as they" (v. 47). Then,

when the apostle was "called on the carpet" by the church leaders in Jerusalem, he declared, "God gave them the like gift as he did unto us, who believed on the Lord Jesus Christ" (Acts 11:17). This last statement leaves no doubt that the glossolalia of Acts 10 was the same in nature as that of Acts 2. Luke uses the word *isēn* ("equal") to describe the gift. The Gentiles are thus treated as equal to the Jews in that both were given the same gift.[2] There is nothing lacking in the Gentile experience which would place it on a level lower than that of the Jews on the day of Pentecost.

Tongues and John's Disciples (Acts 19:1-7)

The third passage in Acts which contains explicit reference to glossolalia is an account of Paul's encounter with twelve disciples of John the Baptist. They had received John's message of expectation which looked forward to the coming of Christ, but they apparently had not been told that Christ had already come, nor did they know anything of the subsequent advent of the Holy Spirit (Acts 19:2). When Paul provided them with fuller information concerning these matters they were baptized. Then Paul laid his hands upon them and "the Holy Ghost came on them; and they spake with tongues, and prophesied" (19:6).

Now, there is no explicit statement that these tongues were foreign languages, nor is there any declaration that the experience was the same as those of Acts 2 or Acts 10. However, inasmuch as Luke uses the same term (*glōssa*) as he uses in the other two accounts, and inasmuch as he does not distinguish between this experience and those of the other two passages, it is necessary that we understand that the phenomenon is

[2]Gustav Stahlin, *"Isos, isotēs, isotimos," Theological Dictionary of the New Testament,* III, 348-49.

the same in Acts 19 as in Acts 2 and 10. In all three cases it was the miracle of speaking in foreign languages not learned by the natural educative process.

Misuse of Tongues at Corinth (I Cor. 12:1—14:40)

In 12:10 Paul says that the Spirit gives "divers kinds of tongues" (*genē glōssōn*) to some believers. The same expression again occurs in 12:28. Then the apostle asks, "Do all speak with tongues [*glōssais*]?" (v. 30). Here there is no indication at all as to the nature of the tongues to which Paul refers.

In I Corinthians 13:1 we read of the tongues of men (*tais glōssais tōn anthrōpōn*) and of angels (*tōn aggelōn*). There is no reason to question the meaning of the phrase "tongues of men"; they are, no doubt, the various languages used by the nations of the world. However, the expression "tongues of angels" seems to describe angelic languages and has been interpreted as referring to an ecstatic type of glossolalia which no one can understand without the gift of interpretation (I Cor. 12:10). These, then, would be heavenly languages rather than foreign languages current among men. The so-called "unknown tongues" of I Corinthians 14 are consequently viewed by many as being these heavenly, angelic languages of I Corinthians 13:1.

However, there is nothing in either chapter 13 or 14 which demands such an interpretation. Although we may grant—as it seems necessary to do—that the tongues of angels are angelic languages, there is no indication that the "unknown tongue" of chapter 14 is an angelic language. In fact, study of that chapter will point out reasons why it should not be identified as such.

It is best to understand Paul as speaking hypothetically and in hyperbole, in which case he would be saying, "Although I speak in the tongues of men and even of angels, it is of absolutely no value if my speech is not bathed in love. No matter how exalted the languages which I may use, they are worthless without love."

Many Bible scholars have interpreted the tongues of I Corinthians 14 as ecstatic utterances in heavenly languages not current in any country on this earth. Others say that both foreign languages and ecstatic languages are in view.

It should be noted first of all that the term "unknown," which occurs in verses 2, 4, 13, 14, 19 and 27, does not occur in any Greek manuscripts. Paul does not say that the tongue is unknown; consequently it is possible that the languages referred to were foreign languages known and used by the various nations of earth. In that case the languages were merely unknown to the people of Corinth just as the Arabic, Urdu, Danish and Russian languages are not familiar to the average church member in America today.

There is nothing in this chapter which requires that ecstatic heavenly languages be found here. The statement that the uninterpreted tongue speaks only to God (v. 2) demands nothing more than a foreign language which the hearer does not understand. The statement that he who speaks in an uninterpreted tongue only edifies himself (v. 4) does not demand an ecstatic heavenly language. Such a speaker edifies no one else because the language used is as foreign to the hearers as Urdu is to the average American. He does, however, edify himself, not because he understands the content of what he says, but because he is aware of the fact that God is performing a miracle in and through him. Such edification, although not on the same intellectual plane as that which comes by means of a known language, is nevertheless an existential and experiential reality. And this is equally true whether the tongue be an ecstatic heavenly language or a foreign earthly language.

In verses 10-11 Paul explains:

> There are, it may be, so many kinds of voices in the world, and none of them is without signification. Therefore if I know not the meaning of the voice, I shall be unto him that speaketh a barbarian, and he that speaketh shall be a barbarian unto me.

The use of the word "voice" may seem confusing at first glance, but it need not be. It is the translation of the Greek *phōnē*, which carries the primary meaning of "sound." In numerous places the word is used in the sense of "voice." However, there are passages in both nonbiblical and biblical Greek where the word means "language." Arndt and Gingrich refer to such uses in Aeschylus, Herodotus, and Diogenes Laertius. Also in the Papyri Graecae Magicae *phōnē* is placed alongside *glōssa* as referring to the same thing.[3] It seems clear, therefore, that Paul is speaking of languages in use "in the world" (v. 10), and this is substantiated by the use of the term "barbarian" (v. 11). The languages are not heavenly in nature; they are the languages of this world, each of which has meaning that is understood by those who know the language.

Further evidence that Paul is referring to foreign languages is found in verse 21 where he says, "In the law it is written, With men of other tongues and other

[3]W. F. Arndt and F. W. Gingrich, *A Greek-English Lexicon of the New Testament,* pp. 878-79.

lips will I speak to this people; and yet for all that they will not hear me, saith the Lord." The Old Testament quotation is from Isaiah 28:11-12, where the prophet is warning God's people of impending judgment at the hands of the Assyrians. Since the people of Israel would not listen to the Lord, they were to be taught their lesson by those who spoke a foreign language. The fact that Paul applies this passage, with its reference to the Assyrian language, to the tongues problem in Corinth is not without significance. It would seem to indicate that the Corinthian tongues were also foreign languages.

It should be noted that one of the component parts of *heteroglōssois* ("other tongues," v. 21) is the word *glōssa* ("tongue"), which is employed elsewhere in the chapter to refer to the gift of tongues.

Since Paul does not distinguish between this use of the word "tongues" and the other uses in the chapter, it is to be assumed that all refer to the same thing, namely, foreign languages. Furthermore, the two component parts of *heteroglōssois* occur separately in the account of the advent of tongues on the day of Pentecost. Luke says, "And they were all filled with the Holy Ghost, and began to speak with other tongues [*heterais glōssais*], as the Spirit gave them utterance" (Acts 2:4). As shown before, it is certain that the Pentecost experience was the miracle of speaking in unlearned foreign languages. It is therefore most reasonable to understand the tongues of I Corinthians 14 to be of the same nature as the tongues of Acts 2.

Luke was a close companion of the Apostle Paul, and there is evidence that as such he was definitely influenced by the theology and terminology of the great apostle. It is certain, for example, that Luke's gospel contains reflections of Pauline theology, such as the use of the term "justified" in Luke 18:14. It is therefore to be expected that Luke would use the word "tongue" (*glōssa*) in the same sense as Paul did. In fact, it is probable that Luke was following Paul's instruction concerning the nature of the gift. And we can be sure that Luke learned about the tongues recorded in Acts 19:1-7 from Paul himself.

Furthermore, if there were a difference in nature between the tongues of Acts and those of Corinthians, both Paul and Luke would no doubt have indicated the distinction in their writings. However, since they do not make such a distinction it is most natural to assume that all valid glossolalia in the New Testament church was foreign-language speaking. The term "tongue" (*glōssa*) had come to have a fixed technical meaning in the early church. S. Lewis Johnson writes:

> In other words, it is most likely that the early believers used a fixed terminology in describing this gift, a terminology understood by them all. If this is so, the full description of the gift on Pentecost must be allowed to explain the more limited descriptions that occur elsewhere.[4]

[4]S. Lewis Johnson, "The Gift of Tongues and the Book of Acts," *Bibliotheca Sacra*, CXX (Oct.-Dec., 1963), 311.

2

The Purpose of Glossolalia

Why should a person desire to speak in a language which he does not know and say things which he himself does not understand? Why would God impart such a gift to a person? What practical purpose can such a strange phenomenon serve? Several answers have been offered for questions such as these.

An Evangelistic Purpose

Some have held that the purpose was to expedite the preaching of the gospel by overcoming the language barrier. The gift, according to this view, was a permanent endowment with a knowledge of the foreign languages needed to preach the gospel.[1] If one could proclaim the message of Christ in a foreign language without taking time to learn that language, consider how much time would be saved and how many more people could be reached.

It is thought that the occurrence of glossolalia on the day of Pentecost (Acts 2) gives evidence favoring this view. The disciples, it is argued, could speak to all of the persons gathered there without being hampered by language differences. One must, however, not overlook the fact that there were two languages which served as international languages of trade and diplo-

[1]Dawson Walker, *The Gift of Tongues*, pp. 15 ff.

macy in the areas delineated in Acts 2:9-11. Since the days of Alexander the Great (331-323 B.C.) the Greek language had been in use in most of these countries. In addition, the nations of the Fertile Crescent stretching from Egypt through Palestine and down into Mesopotamia knew and used Aramaic as an international language of commerce and diplomacy. Consequently, it was not necessary to use the native languages of the people gathered at Pentecost in order to reach them. Since both the disciples and their hearers understood both Aramaic and Greek the gospel could have been communicated effectively without any supernatural gift of tongues.

A Devotional Purpose

Others have suggested that the purpose of glossolalia was that of worship to God. It is viewed as a more effective means of speaking to God in prayer and praise. This interpretation is based on several Scripture passages. Paul in I Corinthians 14:14-17, 28 speaks of the use of tongues in prayer. When a person prayed in a tongue his spirit prayed although his mind did not understand the content of the prayer ("my understanding is unfruitful," v. 14). If a person prayed in a tongue ("bless with the spirit," v. 16) in a public meeting of the church when no interpreter was present, the person who did not understand the language used ("he that occupieth the room of the unlearned," v. 16) could not participate understandingly in the prayer ("say Amen at thy giving of thanks," v. 16).

Therefore, there are two alternative actions prescribed by Paul: (1) to pray in a tongue which the petitioner understands ("pray with the spirit, and . . . with the understanding also," v. 15) and (2) to re-

strict praying in tongues to private prayer ("let him
speak to himself, and to God," v. 28). In the former
case it is to be assumed that the person understands
what he is praying in a tongue because he has received
the gift of interpretation. This is suggested by the
prayer which Paul prescribes in the immediately pre-
ceding context: "Wherefore let him that speaketh in an
unknown tongue pray that he may interpret" (v. 13).

It is clear that, under the proper circumstances, Paul
does allow for the use of tongues in prayer. However,
it does not appear that this is their primary purpose.
The main concern of Paul in I Corinthians 14 is that
all who hear a public utterance in the church should be
able to understand and thus be edified. When the absence of an interpreter makes this impossible, tongues-
praying is relegated to private use in a manner which
suggests its relative unimportance (v. 28).

The employment of tongues in praying is sometimes
seen in Romans 8:26: "Likewise the Spirit also helpeth
our infirmities: for we know not what we should pray
for as we ought: but the Spirit itself maketh intercession for us with groanings which cannot be uttered."
It is thought that "groanings which cannot be uttered"
refers to our own inability to express the deep spiritual
desires of our hearts. However, notice that it is the
Spirit's intercession for us, not our feeble praying,
which is marked by "groanings which cannot be uttered." Furthermore, these groanings are not vocalized
in speech of any kind, for they "cannot be uttered."
This verse and the following one speak of the Holy
Spirit's intercession, not our verbalized prayer.

Paul's exhortation in Ephesians 5:18-20 is also cited
as grounds for using tongues in worship. Here the
apostle writes:

> And be not drunk with wine, wherein is excess;
> but be filled with the Spirit; speaking to your-
> selves in psalms and hymns and spiritual songs,
> singing and making melody in your heart to the
> Lord; giving thanks always for all things unto God
> and the Father in the name of our Lord Jesus
> Christ.

We have previously pointed out, however, that although the filling of the Spirit is urged and speaking
is mentioned, nothing is said about glossolalia. Speaking with tongues can only be found here when one reads
it into the passage. The same is true of the parallel
statement in Colossians 3:16.

From this survey, then, we may conclude that the
primary purpose of tongues was not for use in worship.
Although they were employed in prayer and praise,
these were merely secondary purposes. We must look
elsewhere in order to discover the main reason for the
gift of glossolalia.

An Evidential Purpose

Several passages clearly indicate that tongues were
signs given primarily to serve an evidential purpose.
This seems to be their function on the day of Pentecost
(Acts 2). The phenomenon of tongues attracted a
crowd (v. 6). It amazed the people when they heard
the disciples speaking in languages which the latter did
not know (vv. 6-8, 12). It served as a springboard for
Peter's sermon (vv. 16-21). And it played a significant
part in the remarkable result of that sermon, the response of three thousand persons to the gospel call (v.
41). And, what is more, Peter explicitly used the miracle of tongues in an evidential manner (vv. 32-36).
Glossolalia ("this, which ye now see and hear," v. 33*b*)

is proof that Christ was raised from the dead and exalted to God's right hand (vv. 32-33).

The author of the book of Hebrews also speaks of the evidential purpose of tongues. In 2:3-4 he says:

> How shall we escape, if we neglect so great salvation; which at first began to be spoken by the Lord, and was confirmed unto us by them that heard him; God also bearing them witness, both with signs and wonders, and with divers miracles, and gifts of the Holy Ghost, according to his own will?

The eyewitnesses who passed on the facts of this great salvation were, for the most part, the apostles of Christ, and these verses inform us that their declarations were accompanied and confirmed by miraculous evidences. The terms used to indicate the nature of these evidences are: signs (*sēmeiois*), wonders (*terasin*), miracles (*dynamesin*) and gifts (*merismois*). All of these phenomena were of a miraculous nature and were intended to confirm the word of the eyewitnesses. They are called signs because they graphically signified the truth which was being declared. They were wonders in that they caused the viewers to wonder or to be amazed (cf. Acts 2:6-8, 12). They are designated as miracles because they were the result of supernatural power (*dynamis*). To this collection of evidential terms the author adds "gifts of the Holy Ghost," which must therefore also be evidential in their significance. The term translated "gifts" is *merismois* which refers to a distribution or apportionment. According to Paul in I Corinthians 12:4-11 the Holy Spirit in sovereign action distributes the various spiritual gifts as He pleases. "But all these worketh that one and selfsame Spirit, dividing to every man severally as he will" (v.

11). And among the gifts distributed by the Spirit is glossolalia (v. 10). Tongues therefore, according to Hebrews 2:3-4, are evidential in purpose.

The gift of tongues falls into the same category as miracles in general, which were most certainly evidential in their primary intent. Although it is true that almost all of the miracles of the New Testament benefited the persons involved, it is clear that their overarching purpose was to authenticate the gospel message and its messenger. In addition to the statement in Hebrews 2:3-4, we may cite Acts 2:22: "Ye men of Israel, hear these words; Jesus of Nazareth, a man approved of God among you by miracles and wonders and signs, which God did by him in the midst of you, as ye yourselves also know." Notice the occurrence of the same three terms as were found in Hebrews 2—miracles, wonders and signs. These three Greek terms also occur in II Corinthians 12:12 where miracles are called "signs [sēmeia] of an apostle," that is, the phenomena which provided divine accreditation of Paul as an apostle.

In John's gospel the term "sign" (sēmeion) is used repeatedly to designate the various miracles performed by Christ. Then, in stating his purpose, John makes clear how he is using the term.

> And many other signs truly did Jesus in the presence of his disciples, which are not written in this book: but these are written, that ye might believe that Jesus is the Christ, the Son of God; and that believing ye might have life through his name (John 20:30-31).

The signs, as employed by John, are evidential in purpose. Thus in the writings of John, Luke, Paul and the author of Hebrews, signs (*sēmeia*) are used to accredit the man of God and his message as being from God.

The gift of tongues not only is associated with such evidential terms as are discussed above, but Paul specifically calls speaking in tongues a sign (*sēmeion*). He says:

> In the law it is written, With men of other tongues and other lips will I speak unto this people; and yet for all that will they not hear me, saith the Lord. Wherefore tongues are for a sign, not to them that believe, but to them that believe not: but prophesying serveth not for them that believe not, but for them which believe (I Cor. 14: 21-22).

In the Old Testament passage quoted by Paul the foreign language of the Assyrians was to serve as a judgmental sign to the Israelites, a proof that God was chastening His people through oppression by their enemies. It is not, however, necessary that we understand that Paul means that New Testament tongues are judgmental in their purpose. What the apostle does say is that tongues in the New Testament, just as in Isaiah 28:11-12, are a sign (*sēmeion*) to unbelievers.

A study of the occurrences of glossolalia in Acts reveals that tongues were employed as evidence of several different facts. In Acts 2 the purpose was clearly to convince the unsaved. Unbelieving Jews were attracted and the claims of the gospel were confirmed to them by the miracle of glossolalia. In this case the tongues preceded the response of repentance and faith (2:4-13, 37-41).

In Acts 10, however, the situation is somewhat different. Here the tongues follow Peter's message (10:44-46). On this occasion the sign seems to be acting in reverse, for it is not the believers who speak in tongues and convince the unbelievers. It is those who had been unbelievers who speak in tongues and convince the believers. Furthermore, tongues here seem to follow belief rather than precede it. Apparently the people in Cornelius' house responded to Peter's message in their hearts, and then they spoke in tongues.

It was therefore not possible for tongues to serve as evidence to these Gentile unbelievers leading to their conversion. Instead tongues functioned as evidence to Peter and his Jewish companions that God was performing the unexpected—He was saving uncircumcised Gentiles through faith alone. It was the irrefutable logic of glossolalia which convinced Peter that these new believers should be baptized (10:47), and it was the same convincing argument that silenced the critical Jewish Christians in Jerusalem (Acts 11:1-2, 15-18). Tongues in Acts 10, then, were evidential, but not intended to convince the unsaved, as in Acts 2. They were evidence for unbelieving Jewish Christians who did not believe that God's redemptive program included uncircumcised Gentiles.

Again, in Acts 19:1-7 the situation is still different. In this case disciples of John the Baptist spoke in tongues. They had received John's message of the coming Messiah and been baptized with John's bapitsm of repentance (vv. 3-4). When Paul explained Christian baptism they were baptized in the name of the Lord Jesus (v. 5). This indicates clearly that they had believed and were saved. However, it was not until Paul laid his hands on them that these believers spoke with tongues and prophesied (v. 6).

It is plain that tongues on this occasion did not function as a sign leading to the conversion of these persons, as in Acts 2. Furthermore, the tongues did not serve to convince Paul of any fact which he had not yet been willing to receive, as in the case of Peter in Acts 10. It remains that glossolalia in Acts 19 must have been evidence offered to John's disciples demonstrating the reality of the Holy Spirit's ministry in their lives. Previous to this occasion they not only had not received the Spirit, but they had not even been aware of His indwelling ministry (v. 2).

In summary, it may be said that the primary purpose of glossolalia was evidential. It was given in the opening days of the Christian era to provide an auspicious launching for the new movement. It was God's stamp of approval on the church and on its message, intended to attract and convince unbelievers. The phenomenon, however, was not limited to the unsaved. God also employed it as evidence for the saved to convince them of truth which they had not previously known or received.

3

The Duration of Glossolalia

Evidence from Church History

A study of church history shows that the gift of tongues (genuine or otherwise) gradually died out except for infrequent occurrences among radical or fringe groups.

One of the earliest of the church Fathers to speak of tongues was Irenaeus who lived about A.D. 140-203. In his day it appears that there were reports of people who had the gifts of tongues and prophecy. He wrote:

> For this reason does the apostle declare, "We speak wisdom among them that are perfect," terming those persons "perfect" who have received the Spirit of God, and who through the Spirit of God do speak in all languages, as he used himself also to speak. In like manner we do also hear many brethren in the Church who possess prophetic gifts, and who through the Spirit speak all kinds of languages, and bring to light for the general benefit the hidden things of men, and declare the mysteries of God, whom also the apostle terms "spiritual."[1]

Tertullian also, who lived about A.D. 150-222, seems to have known of people who had similar gifts. In his refutation of the heretic Marcion he wrote:

[1]Irenaeus, "Against Heresies," V. 6. 1.

Let Marcion then exhibit, as gifts of his god,
some prophets, such as have not spoken by human
sense, but with the Spirit of God, such as have
both predicted things to come, and have made
manifest the secrets of the heart; let him produce
a psalm, a vision, a prayer—only let it be by the
Spirit, in an ecstasy, that is, in a rapture, when-
ever an interpretation of tongues has occurred to
him. . . . Now all these signs (of spiritual gifts)
are forthcoming from my side without any difficulty.[2]

Does Tertullian really say that there were people in his
day who possessed the spiritual gifts to which he refers?
Not necessarily! He is only saying that he can cite the
existence of such gifts among Christians. He does not
say when these gifts appeared. Perhaps he was referring to the presence of miraculous gifts in the apostolic
age as proofs of the validity of Christianity. However,
if it be insisted that Tertullian was in reality referring
to spiritual gifts being exercised during his lifetime, it
should be pointed out that the above statement was
made after he had joined the ranks of the Montanists.[3]
This schismatic movement, which had its origin in
Phrygia, believed in the continued existence of miraculous spiritual gifts. Both Montanus and his two fe-
male associates insisted that they were mouthpieces of
the Holy Spirit who had revealed to them that the New
Jerusalem would soon descend from heaven and be
located in Phrygia.[4]

Chrysostom (A.D. 347-407) leaves no doubt that in
his day tongues were altogether a thing of the past.
Writing concerning I Corinthians 12, he said: "This

[2]Tertullian, "Against Marcion," V. 8.
[3]Alexander Roberts and James Donaldson, *The Ante-Nicene
Fathers*, III, 11.
[4]Kenneth S. Latourette, *A History of Christianity*, p. 128.

whole place is very obscure: but the obscurity is produced by our ignorance of the facts referred to and by their cessation, being such as then used to occur, but now no longer take place."[5]

And Augustine, who was a contemporary of Chrysostom living from A.D. 354 to 430, was equally definite. He said:

> In the earliest times, "the Holy Ghost fell upon them that believed: and they spake with tongues," which they had not learned, "as the Spirit gave them utterance." These were signs adapted to the time. For there behooved to be that betokening of the Holy Spirit in all tongues, to shew that the Gospel of God was to run through all tongues over the whole earth. That thing was done for a betokening, and it passed away.[6]

From this time on in the history of the church until the advent of modern Pentecostalism, glossolalia is reported with notable infrequency, and then generally in groups whose character gives reason for suspecting the validity of the report or of the phenomenon reported. Writing in "A Symposium on Speaking in Tongues," Harris Kaasa says:

> In summary we may say that there is considerable evidence for the recurrence of this phenomenon. At the same time, no one can fail to be struck by its relative infrequency and by the fact that it occurs mostly among members of (in context) radical sects. It exceptional presence should not blind us to its general absence in the main stream of church history.[7]

[5]Chrysostom, "Homilies on the First Epistle of Paul the Apostle to the Corinthians," XXIX.

[6]Augustine, "Homilies on the First Epistle of John," VI. 10.

[7]Harris Kaasa, "An Historical Evaluation" in "A Symposium on Speaking in Tongues," *Dialog,* II (Spring, 1963), 157.

A common Pentecostal explanation of the cessation of tongues in the church has been that this was brought about by the increasing spiritual decline which took place beginning as early as the end of the apostolic age. And it must be granted that such a declension did occur. Christ, for example, rebuked the Ephesian church saying, "Thou hast left thy first love" (Rev. 2:4). What was true of Ephesus became increasingly true of the church at large, but through the years in a church which has left much to be desired spiritually there have been towering spiritual giants who surely have met the requirements for reception of the gift of tongues. If it had been in the plan of God to impart this gift throughout this age, surely men like Augustine, Luther, George Mueller, Charles G. Finney and D. L. Moody were qualified to receive it. The fact is that they did not. It does not appear therefore that declining spirituality was the reason for the cessation of tongues in the church.

Evidence from Scripture

At this point we may rightly ask whether or not the New Testament gives any indication concerning the duration of glossolalia. Many have cited I Corinthians 13:8 as proof that tongues would cease, and there can be no doubt but that this verse does explicitly declare the cessation of this gift. Paul says: "Love never fails; but if there are gifts of prophecy, they will be done away; if there are tongues, they will cease; if there is knowledge, it will be done away" (NASB). We must notice, however, that this verse does not say that tongues were to cease at the end of the apostolic age. In fact, it allows for the existence of tongues until "that which is perfect" has come (v. 10), and then "shall I

know even as also I am known" (v. 12). The verb
epiginōskō in verse 12 speaks of full knowledge, and
the general sense of the verse points, not to an experience of this life or this age, but to the time when salvation is complete and we see Christ "as he is" (I John
3:2). Then there will be no more place for tongues or
prophecy for knowledge will be complete. To make
I Corinthians 13:8 prove that God intended glossolalia
to cease at the end of the apostolic age is to violate the
valid rules of biblical interpretation in the interest of a
previously determined position.

Does the New Testament have anything to say concerning the cessation of tongues at the end of the
apostolic age? In searching for an answer to this question, consider I Corinthians 12:28 where Paul has listed
a number of functionaries and functions which God has
placed in the church: "And God hath set some in the
church, first apostles, secondarily prophets, thirdly
teachers, after that miracles, then gifts of healings,
helps, governments, diversities of tongues."

Was it the divine intention that all of these items
should continue in the church throughout the age? It
is to be noted that both apostles and tongues are included on an equal plane in this list. An examination
of the New Testament and early church history reveals
that the apostolic office was not a continuing feature of
the early church. It did cease. Whereas the apostles
were careful to choose a successor for Judas in the days
immediately following Christ's ascension (Acts 1:15
ff.), there is no indication that any further attempt was
made to choose successors for the apostles. When
James died as the second martyr no replacement was
selected (Acts 12:1 ff.). When Paul spoke of his approaching death he gave no instructions concerning a

successor (II Tim. 4:6-8). In fact, by the very nature
of the apostolic office it could not be extended indef-
initely, for it required persons who had been witnesses
of the resurrection (Acts 1:21-22). Thus, when John
passed off the scene about the end of the first century
the office of the apostle ceased to exist.

It is evident, then, that one of the items listed by
Paul in I Corinthians 12:28 did cease long before the
end of the church age. If one member of Paul's list
was withdrawn, it is at least possible that other items
may have been withdrawn as well.

In Ephesians 2:20 Paul links the prophet with the
apostle and characterizes both as foundational in re-
lation to the church: ". . . and are built upon the
foundation of the apostles and prophets." This suggests that both apostles and prophets belong to the
foundation period of the church rather than to the
time when the superstructure is being erected. Not only
was the apostle temporary in the plan of God, but it
also appears that the prophet likewise did not continue.

But what about the other items on Paul's list? No
one would argue that the teaching office ceased, but
what can be said of miracles and healing? In II Corinthians 12:12 miracles are clearly associated with the
apostle as a divine accreditation. Paul says, "Truly
the signs of an apostle were wrought among you in all
patience, in signs, and wonders, and mighty deeds."
In some sense Paul views miracles as being related to
the apostolic office. Like the apostle and prophet, they
were foundational in nature. They were used to give
God's stamp of approval to the new movement, the
New Testament church. The Lord launched His church
with an auspicious program which included the testi-

mony of eyewitnesses and the presence of the miraculous. The aim was to confirm the trustworthiness of the claim that the incarnate Son of God had procured salvation from sin for all who would receive it.

The author of Hebrews, writing in the second generation after the cross, said:

> How shall we escape, if we neglect so great salvation; which at first began to be spoken by the Lord, and was confirmed unto us by them that heard him; God also bearing them witness, both with signs and wonders, and with divers miracles, and gifts of the Holy Ghost, according to his own will? (Heb. 2:3-4).

The verb "was confirmed" (v. 3) is the Greek aorist *ebebaiōthē* which, in this and most cases, is equivalent to our simple past. The confirmation was a past event and so also was the corroborative witness which God provided in the form of miracles and gifts of the Holy Spirit (v. 4). This is evident because the Greek present tense participle "bearing witness" (*synepimartyrountos*) describes action contemporaneous with that of the main verb "was confirmed" (*ebebaiōthē*). Thus, when the author of Hebrews wrote, both the eyewitness testimony and the miraculous corroboration were past events. The verb tenses do not indicate that these things were still in process of occurring.

In the early days of the New Testament church, while it was in process of laying its foundations, God used eyewitnesses and miracles to establish the new structure in preparation for its age-long task. After those foundations were firmly planted, and after the New Testament Scriptures were produced and placed in circulation as the sure Word of God, then the apostolic office passed away, and with it the miraculous events which had served as apostolic credentials.

It is true that claims have been made for the continuation of miracles through the years, but what are called miracles today are in most cases a far cry from the instantaneous healings and resuscitations of the New Testament. Although God may perform a miracle at any time He in His sovereignty chooses to do so, it is not the divine order for this age.

It is clear from Hebrews 2:3-4 that miracles in general and tongues in particular both served the same purpose. They were used to corroborate the message being proclaimed by the apostles and their colleagues. Not only were miracles and tongues the same in purpose; they were also the same in nature for glossolalia was itself a miracle. To be able to speak in another language which one has never learned is as miraculous as walking on the sea or healing the sick. Consequently, it is natural that when miracles passed off the scene, tongues also disappeared.

This is not to say that all of the charismatic gifts ceased. The gifts of the Spirit fall into two categories: those which are miraculous in an objective sense and thus evidential, and those which are miraculous only in a subjective sense (word of wisdom, word of knowledge, faith, discerning of spirits, I Cor. 12:8-10). At the end of the apostolic age, the former category of gifts gradually ceased to be the order of the day. This included healings, tongues, interpretation of tongues, prophecy and other gifts which may have been objectively miraculous in nature. Such things did not fade away because of the sagging spiritual life of the church, as Pentecostals claim, but rather because they had fulfilled their purpose in the divine plan for the age.

MISUSE OF GLOSSOLALIA
IN CORINTH

4

The Problem

In our day I Corinthians 12-14 has been variously treated. By some Pentecostal groups the controls here set forth seem to have been almost completely overlooked. On the other hand some who oppose Pentecostal beliefs and practices use these chapters to disprove the Pentecostal position. It is therefore important that we seek objectively to discover both what the situation was which occasioned this passage and what Paul really is saying in response to that situation.

What the Corinthian Phenomenon Was Not

In order to avoid approaching the passage with misconceptions, it is advisable at the very beginning to set aside certain possible misinterpretations. Such a procedure will enable us to see more clearly what the Corinthian problem was and what Paul has to say concerning it.

First, these chapters give no indication at all that speaking in tongues was wrong or that the Corinthians were engaging in a forbidden activity. Paul does not criticize his readers for practicing tongues. He does not deny that what they were doing was a gift of the Holy Spirit. He makes no claim that it was not real, that it was put on or that it was the result of undue emotionalism. Rather than forbidding tongues as invalid, he closes his instructions concerning the subject with the prohibition "Forbid not to speak with tongues" (I Cor. 14:39). The apostle does not indicate that the Corinthians were speaking in some sort of ecstatic gibberish, whereas the genuine gift of tongues was the ability to speak in actual foreign languages as on the day of Pentecost (Acts 2:1-11). There is nothing in the chapter which suggests that the *nature* of the Corinthian glossolalia was perverted in any way.

It may be argued that what Paul has to say about musical instruments which give uncertain sounds or sounds with no distinction (I Cor. 14:7 ff.) suggests that the Corinthian tongues were gibberish which could not be understood by anyone. Such an interpretation, however, reads an idea into the passage which is not in keeping with the context. Paul is asserting that tongues are only useful in the church if what is said can be understood by those who hear (v. 6). If the hearers do not understand what is said, the speaker is like a foreigner ("barbarian") to them (v. 11). Even musical instruments give forth understandable sounds, so that the trumpet can alert the soldier to prepare for battle (vv. 7-8). How much more should the person who speaks in the church speak in a language which people can understand (vv. 9, 12). Paul is not accusing the Corinthians of speaking in "jabberwocky" or "gobbledegook." Nor is he urging them to use legitimate languages rather than gibberish when they exercise the gift of tongues. He is merely instructing them to use a language which makes sense to the hearers or, if they do speak in a foreign tongue, to be sure that an interpreter is present to explain the meaning of the tongues-speech to those who listen.

Second, note that Paul does not say, as some assume,

that speaking in tongues in private is either useless or
wrong. When he forbids the public use of tongues, Paul
does not likewise forbid private use. He says, "But if
there be no interpreter, let him keep silence in the
church; and let him speak to himself, and to God"
(I Cor. 14:28).

Furthermore, he explicitly declares that he who
speaks in a tongue edifies himself (I Cor. 14:4). It has
been suggested that the person who is self-edified is one
who understands the language which he is using; but
this cannot be, for then he would be able to interpret
the utterance and thus edify the church. Paul is saying
that there is personal edification for the glossolalist
even though he does not understand the meaning of his
speech. Exactly how he is edified or built up spiritually is not stated. It may be assumed that the experience of the miracle of tongues is understood as
being from God, and the speaker is thus edified. It may
be that the sense of the presence of God, although the
tongues-speech is not understood, is of spiritual benefit to the speaker. But whatever may be the apostle's
meaning, it is certain that there is some value in the
private use of tongues. Such a practice is not forbidden,
nor does Paul speak of it as a kind of spiritual toy employed to secure some sort of selfish emotional thrill.

What the Corinthian Phenomenon Was

It appears that the carnal Corinthian Christians—
for so Paul characterizes them—had allowed their car-
nality to invade the area of spiritual gifts. Even as
there was competition among the factions mentioned
in chapters 1-4, so there was pride and jealousy over
the possession of the gift of tongues. Then, as now, it
apparently had been exalted as the gift *par excellence*

which provided its possessor with a certain spiritual prestige and which placed all others on a lower level of Christian living.

This may be inferred from Paul's discussion of the various members of the body (I Cor. 12:12-30). He is combatting the exaltation of one gift to the exclusion of the others. The whole body, he says, is not an eye, nor is it an ear (v. 17), nor because the foot is not the hand should it assume that it is not part of the body (v. 15), nor should the eye assume that the hand is useless (v. 21). These statements suggest a condition in which it was thought that only one gift really counted and that everybody ought to have it. From the contrast between tongues and prophecy in chapter 14, it is apparent that the overvalued gift was glossolalia. It was the one gift for which everyone longed. Perhaps this was because of its obviously miraculous nature or because of its signal importance stemming back to the beginning on the day of Pentecost. Whatever the explanation, the Corinthians were guilty of an extreme overemphasis on tongues as the most desirable gift of all.

Closely related to this undue exaltation of glossolalia was a serious lack of love, especially in connection with the exercise of the gifts of the Spirit. This deficiency is to be inferred from I Corinthians 13 where the gifts of tongues, prophecy, knowledge, faith and giving are mentioned (13:1-3). The pride engendered by possession of the prestige gift—tongues—was certainly far removed from love. So also was the discrimination practiced against those who had the so-called lesser gifts. The desire to show off one's prestige gift in the assembly, even though it benefited no one present, was in contradiction to the principle of love for the brethren.

The situation which resulted was one of confusion and disorder (14:40) in which many were speaking in tongues and prophesying at the same time (14:27-32). There was no concern that anyone be able to understand what was spoken. People spoke in tongues whether or not an interpreter was present (14:13, 27-28). Women seem to have been involved in this rowdy situation; whether it was in the employment of tongues or merely in conversing out loud with their husbands, we cannot be sure (14:34-35).

In all that Paul has to say concerning the tongues disorder at Corinth, he nowhere denies the validity nor reality of the gift as exercised there. Nor does he say anything which would demand that the gift be understood as anything different from the supernatural ability to speak in unlearned foreign languages as in Acts 2. The problem in Corinth was simply an unloving overemphasis on tongues which resulted in confusion in the public services of the church and division in the body of Christ (12:25).

5

The Pauline Corrective

Paul's purpose in I Corinthians 12-14 is not to forbid the exercise of tongues; it is to correct the misuse of a legitimate gift. His approach to the problem is a discussion of spiritual gifts in general in order that tongues may be seen in the larger context of gifts as a whole.

The Doctrine of Spiritual Gifts (I Cor. 12)

The Corinthian believers needed to understand that there was a variety of gifts, but all were given by the same Spirit (12:4-11). Furthermore, Paul insists, the Spirit is sovereign in His distribution of the gifts. He distributes them "to each one individually just as He wills" (12:11, NASB). Hence, if one person receives the gift of knowledge, it is because the Holy Spirit Himself has chosen to give it to him. If another receives the gift of tongues, it is because of the sovereign decision of the Spirit. If still another possesses the gift of healing, it is because this is the Spirit's will for that person. Consequently, no one should deprecate himself as spiritually inferior because he has received the gift of knowledge rather than tongues. The kind of gift a person receives is not a gauge of spirituality; it is instead an indication of the free and independent will of the Spirit of God.

Whereas in Corinth the question of gifts had produced division of the Christian community, Paul proceeds to make it clear that gifts are intended not to divide but to unify the church by meeting the needs of the body as a whole (12:12-27). Unity of the body is served by the diversity of the gifts. As each part of the body is dependent upon every other part, so each member of the church is dependent upon every other member and his particular gift (12:12-21). No part of the body is unnecessary. In fact, the less attractive members of the body may be more valuable. Just so, gifts which may not be so striking may be more significant for the spiritual welfare of the whole church than the more showy gifts (12:22-24). Tongues, to be sure, were a remarkable demonstration of supernatural activity, but the word of knowledge (12:8), for example, was of more benefit to the church in its entirety. Thus, all of the members should have concern for each individual member, and each individual member should be concerned for all of the other members, for they belong one to another and they exist for each other's benefit (12:25-26).

In concluding chapter 12 Paul indicates by a series of questions that no gift is a required possession for all believers (vv. 29-30). Each of these questions clearly expects a negative reply. "Are all apostles?" Obviously not! "Are all workers of miracles?" Certainly not! And by the same token not all are intended to speak in tongues.

Nearly all would agree that the tongues of I Corinthians were not intended for every Christian. However, many Pentecostals make a distinction between the tongues which come as a sign of baptism with the Holy Spirit, and thus occur but once, and the gift of tongues

which is a continuing possession. Every believer, they
say, can and should be baptized in the Holy Spirit and
manifest the same by speaking in tongues. On the other
hand, in addition to the initial experience at the time
of Spirit baptism, the Spirit gives the continuing gift
of speaking in tongues. It is the claim of Pentecostals
that the initial experience of tongues is the type of
glossolalia seen in Acts 2, 10 and 19. The continuing
gift is said to be the kind of glossolalia discussed in
I Corinthians 12–14.[1]

In reply, it should first be pointed out that in I Corinthians 12:13 Paul declares that all believers, even
the carnal Corinthians, have been baptized by the Holy
Spirit. The apostle does not command Christians to
be baptized by the Spirit; he declares it to be a fact that
all of them *are* already baptized with the Spirit. And
the verse leaves no doubt as to when this occurs. It is
simultaneous with the believer's introduction into the
body of Christ, the church.

It is noteworthy that the baptism of I Corinthians
12:13 is tied to the promised baptism of Acts 1:5 by the
use of the same Greek preposition. In Acts Jesus said,
"Ye shall be baptized with [*en*] the Holy Ghost." In
Corinthians Paul says, "By [*en*] one Spirit are we all
baptized." The Greek preposition *en* may be used with
the locative case to mean "in," but it is also often used
with the instrumental case to mean "with" or "by means
of." Although it is possible to understand *en* as meaning "in" in Acts 1:5 and "by" in I Corinthians 12:13,
it is more consistent to interpret both occurrences of
the word in the instrumental sense. Believers are baptized with or by the Holy Spirit. We must conclude,

[1]Carl Brumback, "What Meaneth This?" *A Pentecostal Answer to a Pentecostal Question,* pp. 261-72.

then, that the baptism with the Spirit is experienced by every believer, that it is experienced but once, and that it always occurs at the time of salvation.

Furthermore, in reply to the Pentecostal assertion, notice that neither in I Corinthians nor in Acts do all who receive the Holy Spirit speak with tongues. In I Corinthians 12:13 all are said to be baptized with the Spirit, but in 12:30 it is implied that not all exercise glossolalia. In Acts 2:38 Peter stated that if his hearers repented and were baptized they would receive the gift of the Holy Spirit, and three thousand of them responded. However, the record says nothing about tongues occurring as a proof that they had received the Spirit. In Acts 8 there is a clear instance of the reception of the Holy Spirit (v. 17), but there is no record that glossolalia followed this experience. Surely in this context of "miracles and signs" (v. 13) Luke would have mentioned the sign of tongues if it had occurred. On the occasion of Saul's conversion (Acts 9:17-19) he was filled with the Holy Spirit (cf. Acts 2:4-5), and yet nothing is said about any manifestation of tongues. It is plain that there is no sound biblical basis for any distinction between tongues as a sign in Acts and as a gift in Corinthians.

The Indispensable Complement of All Gifts
(I Cor. 13)

Returning to I Corinthians we note that Paul has injected into the midst of his discussion of gifts a short but moving discussion of love. Chapter 13 is almost parenthetical. The apostle could have moved directly from 12:31a to 14:1b with an uninterrupted chain of thought. However, this choice chapter setting forth the necessity, the nature, and the permanence of love was introduced to impress on the minds and hearts of the Corinthian believers the fact that love must temper the use of all spiritual gifts or they will be utterly worthless. Without love, the most exalted glossolalia is mere noise. Where love is lacking, the most thorough understanding of God's truth, as well as the most effective faith, are absolutely nothing.

Spiritual gifts cannot properly be used for selfish ends. They must never be employed as means to gain spiritual prestige. They should never produce a haughty attitude of discrimination toward those who may not possess the same supernatural ability. One who had received the gift of tongues was no better than one who possessed the gift of knowledge. Both gifts were imparted for the benefit of the whole Christian community, and love will see to it that they serve the whole community. If love had been in control in the Corinthian church, Paul would not have needed to write these three chapters.

The Control of the Gift of Tongues (I Cor. 14)

Having dealt with spiritual gifts in general (I Cor. 12-13), the apostle then sets his sights on the one particular gift which had become a problem in the church. Chapter 14 treats in a detailed fashion the misuse of the gift of tongues. The basic rule which he lays down is that everything which is done in the public meeting of the church must serve to edify the church ("Let all things be done unto edifying," v. 26). A number of specific regulations flow from this general rule.

First, this principle meant that tongues are not to be sought as the most desirable gift. This may be suggested by the fact that in the three lists of gifts in chapter 12 tongues and their interpretation are in-

variably placed last (vv. 10, 28, 30). That tongues are
not to be desired is also suggested in the command to
"covet earnestly the best gifts" (12:31). But the most
explicit statement occurs in 14:1: "Pursue love, yet
desire earnestly spiritual gifts, but especially that you
may prophesy" (NASB). The next twenty-four verses
are devoted to the demonstration of the superiority of
prophecy over tongues. The basic argument is that
prophecy can be understood directly without an interpreter and thus the hearers are edified, whereas tongues
are not understood unless an interpreter is present (vv.
3-4). Therefore, if any gift is to be sought it should be
the gift of prophecy, not tongues.

The second regulation which the apostle lays down
is that the person who speaks in tongues should pray
for the gift of interpretation (v. 13). Again, the reason
for this command is that interpretation is necessary for
edification of the church.

The third regulation limits the public use of tongues
to those times when an interpreter is present (v. 28).
If there is no interpreter, the tongues-speaker is to
"keep silence in the church." What is meant by this
prohibition may be seen by comparing it with the same
directive addressed to the women (vv. 34-35). They
too are told to "keep silence in the churches." That
this did not mean to speak softly or to whisper is evident from the instruction to "ask their husbands at
home." By the same token uninterpreted tongues were
not to be permitted in the church in any form even
when practiced quietly in a low voice. This regulation
is often violated in Pentecostal circles today, and neo-
Pentecostals are no less guilty. The latter may argue
that small glossolalic groups meeting in homes do not
constitute a church. Although this is true, the require-

ment that tongues must edify the hearers cannot be so narrowly interpreted as applying only to an organized church situation. The principle certainly applies to any group situation where there is no one present who can interpret.

The fourth rule requires that tongues must always be employed in orderly fashion (v. 27). No more than two or three were to speak in tongues on one occasion, and then they were to speak in turn, not all at once (cf. v. 40). Here again, Pentecostals often have overlooked Paul's stipulation, both in the failure to limit speaking to three at the most and in permitting more than one to speak at a time.

The fifth rule applies the same controls to the use of prophecy in the church meeting (vv. 29-33).

In the sixth place, Paul prohibits women from speaking in church (vv. 34-35). Whether this regulation refers to tongues and prophecy we cannot be sure, since neither is specifically mentioned. It may be that women had been speaking out loud to their husbands when they wanted to ask them about something, for Paul says, "If they will learn anything, let them ask their husbands at home" (v. 35).

The seventh rule laid down by the apostle forbids the prohibition of tongues. In a condition of confusion such as existed in the Corinthian church some might have been tempted to forbid tongues altogether, but Paul's solution was not exclusion. It was control.

In his effort to control glossolalia, it is apparent that Paul de-emphasizes the gift both in chapter 12 and in chapter 14. Surely, his reason for playing it down was not merely a pragmatic one—merely to reduce noise and disorder in the church. Such a reason would justify controls, but not deemphasis. It may be that the gift

was played down because of the declining need for it by
A.D. 55 when I Corinthians was written.

More fitting is the explanation which takes into account the evidential purpose of tongues as a sign for
unbelievers to help to convince them of the truthfulness
of the gospel message (I Cor. 14:22). When tongues
were used for any other purpose than this they were
relatively unimportant and should rightly be depre-
ciated.

Paul's controls in I Corinthians 14 were intended to
preserve the evidential value of glossolalia as signs. If
the misuse of tongues was to become commonplace,
they would lose all evidential value as Paul suggests in
I Corinthians 14:23: "If therefore the whole church be
come together into one place, and all speak with
tongues, and there come in those that are unlearned, or
unbelievers, will they not say that ye are mad?" Thus,
when the gift is employed in public, it must be used in
such a way that it has evidential value. Speakers must
speak in turn, they are limited to two or three in number, and an interpreter must be present to make known
what is being said.

If such conditions cannot be met, Paul forbids the
public employment of the gift, relegating it to the obscurity of privacy. There it has the secondary value of
a lower-level edification (I Cor. 14:4).

PRESENT-DAY GLOSSOLALIA

6

An Analysis

When a person asserts that the New Testament gift of tongues as a normal occurrence ceased at the end of the apostolic age, he is required by that denial to explain the current phenomenon which is being designated as biblical tongues. If the Lord is no longer giving the gift of tongues, what is occurring among Pentecostals and neo-Pentecostals today? One cannot fairly deny the continuation of New Testament glossolalia and yet refuse to face up to the present-day phenomenon.

As time passes more material of an objective nature is available as a basis for analysis. The appearance of neo-Pentecostalism on the religious scene has called new attention to glossolalia, with the result that additional analyses have been undertaken. Consequently, we are in a better position today to examine the phenomenon than ever before.

It must be emphasized that our discussion is in no way intended to be unkind or destructively critical. Those who believe that they have received the gift of tongues value the experience highly as being from God. We personally are aware that many of those who use tongues are deeply committed to our Lord and that their desire is to know Him as fully as possible. In no

way are the following pages intended as a depreciation
of such devotion and desire. The author values the
friendship of a number of persons both in Pentecostal
and neo-Pentecostal groups, and he cannot help but re-
spect them as sincere servants of our Lord.

Our analysis includes both the glossolalia currently
occurring among Christians and that which has been
witnessed among non-Christians.

Christian Glossolalia

We have presented evidence for believing that all
New Testament glossolalia was in the nature of miraculous speech in unlearned foreign languages. This was
clearly the case on the day of Pentecost (Acts 2), and
there is no sound basis for viewing the tongues of I Corinthians 12-14 as being anything different. If our interpretation of the Corinthian chapters has been correct, present-day glossolalia, in order to be considered
genuine, must likewise be shown to be the miraculous
use of unlearned foreign languages.

Many claims concerning instances of glossolalia in
foreign languages have been heard. A student recently
told me that he had spoken in perfect Turkish in a
public service. Sometimes bystanders have told tongues-
speakers that their speech "sounded like" Japanese or
Russian. The truth of the matter is that such stories,
though many, are hardly ever subject to verification.

Since the invention of the tape recorder it has become possible to record glossolalic speech for later lin-
guistic analysis by experts in the field. To the author's
knowledge no taped utterance has ever been identified
by qualified linguists as a specific language. Some may
object that not all of the three thousand or more languages in use are known by linguists, and for this rea-

son the taped speeches may not have been recognized. Such an objection is refuted in a letter written to *Christianity Today* by William E. Welmers, Professor of African Languages at the University of California at Los Angeles. He explains:

> We do know something about representative languages of every known language family in the world. I am by no means unique among descriptive linguists in having had direct, personal contact with well over a hundred languages representing a majority of the world's language families, and in having studied descriptions of languages of virtually every reported type. If a glossolalic were speaking in any of the thousand languages of Africa, there is about a 90 per cent chance that I would know it in a minute.[1]

In another *Christianity Today* article, Frank Farrell, one-time assistant editor, relates the results of the analysis of taped tongues-speech by a group of government linguists.[2] The glossolalist whose speech was recorded was the Reverend Harald Bredesen, chairman of the board of the Blessed Trinity Society. The linguists did not recognize the utterance as being any specific language, although one thought that it possessed the structure of a language.

William Welmers likewise reports on an analysis which he made of a sample of tongues-speech. He found the following to be true:

1. There were "no more than two contrasting vowel sounds."

[1]William E. Welmers, letter to *Christianity Today*, VIII (Nov. 8, 1963), 127. Used by permission.
[2]Frank Farrell, "Outburst of Tongues: The New Penetration," *Christianity Today*, VII (Sept. 13, 1963), 1166.

2. There was "a most peculiarly restricted set of consonant sounds."

3. These made up "a very few syllable clusters which recur many times in various orders."

4. The "intonation patterns" are "completely American English." Welmer's conclusion is that the sample "does *not* sound like a language structurally."[3]

In a master's thesis presented to the Hartford Seminary Foundation, Walter A. Wolfram analyzes glossolalic texts of eight primary informants from the viewpoint of structural linguistics. His study reveals the following characteristics:

1. The texts were clearly related to the language backgrounds of the speakers. They had obviously drawn phonemes (speech sounds) from languages with which they were familiar.

2. There are similarities among the speakers which would not be present if they were speaking different languages. These included excessive use of the vowel *a,* a high frequency of open syllables, and a tendency to end breath groups in vowels and often the same vowel.

3. There is a high frequency of repetition of certain words or clauses. One informant repeated the same clause "more than ten times in succession." Some glossolalia is largely made up of a clause repeated over and over. Words, also, are repeated in numerous alternant forms. Two informants employed as many as twenty alternants for one term.[4]

---

[3]Welmers, *ibid.*

[4]Walter A. Wolfram, "The Sociolinguistics of Glossolalia" (unpublished Master's thesis), pp. 91-92.

Wolfram concludes from these characteristics that "it is highly improbable that glossolalists are speaking an unlearned non-native language."[5]

George B. Cutten, in a most thorough treatment of speaking in tongues written forty years ago, found similar characteristics in samples of tongues-speech which he analyzed. He called attention to alliteration and repetition, and he cited the following as examples:

> prou pray praddey,
> pa palassate pa pau pu pe,
> teli terattate taw,
> terrei te te-te-te,
> vole virte vum,
> elee lete leele luto,
> singe sirge singe,
> imba imba imba.[6]

Cutten cites Mosiman, who wrote in 1911, to the effect that, although he had traced many claims of "real speech in foreign languages," he had failed to find one case that was authentic.[7] Cutten also examined many such claims and came to the same conclusion as Mosiman.[8]

Another subject which is related to the question under discussion is that of the interpretation of tongues. If glossolalia is speech in foreign languages, certain translation characteristics will be present. In general it may be said that there will be a certain amount of correspondence between the text of the tongues utterance and the text of the interpretation.

The two texts will not be greatly different in length.

[5]*Ibid.*, p. 91.
[6]George B. Cutten, *Speaking with Tongues Historically and Psychologically Considered*, pp. 174-75.
[7]*Ibid.*, pp. 178-79.
[8]*Ibid.*, pp. 179-81.

However, Welmers found a noticeable difference at this point. He says:

> At the most generous estimate, the glossolalic utterance includes ten or eleven "sentences" or stretches of possible meaningful speech. But the "interpretation" involves no less than fourteen distinct and independent ideas. There simply can be no match between the "tongue" and the "interpretation."[9]

Another factor which militates against the possibility that glossolalia is actual foreign language is the inconsistency seen within given interpretations. Often the same clause when repeated is interpreted to mean something radically different.

Analysts have noted that interpretations are usually couched in an English style which is remarkably similar to that of the King James Version. In addition the content reveals nothing which is not already set forth in the Scriptures. John Oman writes:

> Speaking in tongues is never creative speaking, but when interpreted there are usually exhortations like those of the New Testament Pastoral Epistles. Rational thinking impels one to ask: What is gained by speaking in tongues if one does not produce any original material or new insights into the religious and spiritual life of a Christian?[10]

Although his comment is not very complimentary, G. Travers Sloyer puts his finger on a noticeable characteristic of much that is called interpretation when he says, "If they are interpreted, the English is so vapid

[9]Welmers, p. 128.

[10]John B. Oman, "On 'Speaking in Tongues': A Psychological Analysis," *Pastoral Psychology*, XIV (Dec., 1963), 49.

that one is reminded of the apocryphal human production of Joseph Smith in the Book of Mormon."[11]

On the basis of such investigations and analyses stretching from 1911 to the present we may conclude that the cumulative evidence indicates that present-day glossolalia is not foreign-language speaking. Such a conclusion is based on:

1. The high frequency of repetition in tongues-speaking.
2. The similarity of tongues-speech to the speaker's language background.
3. The excessive use of one or two vowels.
4. The absence of any language structure.
5. The markedly greater length of the interpretation as compared with the tongue utterance.
6. The inconsistency in interpretation of the same clause or phrase.
7. The predominantly King James style employed in interpretations.

In addition, no sample of tongues-speech which has been carefully analyzed by qualified specialists has proved to be an unlearned, nonnative language. It is because of such factors as these that competent linguists who have made investigation do not regard glossolalia as speech in actual languages.

Nonchristian Glossolalia

When considering the phenomenon of glossolalia as it has appeared since New Testament times, it is necessary to give attention briefly to its appearance in nonchristian circumstances. The fact of such appearance

[11]G. Travers Sloyer, *Is This Revival?* p. 10.

may have some bearing on glossolalia as it currently occurs within the Christian church.

L. Carlyle May, in an *American Anthropologist* article entitled "A Survey of Glossolalia and Related Phenomena in Non-Christian Religions," has recorded extensive data concerning tongues, especially as employed by the shaman or priest and medicine man. May points out that speaking the language of supernatural beings while entranced or religiously exalted occurs frequently in healing rituals. An example cited is the woman shaman among the Hudson Bay Eskimos who spoke to the spirits in their own language. In such cases the speaker is supposed to become the mouthpiece of the god, and he does not afterward remember what he has said.[12] The shaman of North Borneo speaks to the celestial spirits in their own language, and in Micronesia in the Mortlock Islands, the spirits are said to open the mouth of the priest and speak through him in a language not his own.[13]

Tongues also are associated with demon possession in various places. D. C. Graham tells of a girl in the Szechwan province of China who was possessed by demons and "began to utter words incoherently."[14] Edward Langston says that in East Africa many persons possessed by demons speak fluently in Swahili or English although under normal circumstances they do not understand either language.[15] Junod reports that

[12]L. Carlyle May, "A Survey of Glossolalia and Related Phenomena in Non-Christian Religions," *American Anthropologist,* LVIII (Feb., 1956), 79.

[13]*Ibid.,* p. 80.

[14]D. C. Graham, *Religion in Szechwan Province, China,* Smithsonian Miscellaneous Collections, LXXX, 4, p. 15, as cited by May, p. 82.

[15]Edward Langston, "What Are Demons?" *The London Quarterly and Holborn Review* (Jan., 1954), p. 30, as cited by May, p. 84.

among the Thonga people of Africa when a demon is being exorcized the person sings a curative song which he himself composes. Usually the songs are in the Zulu tongue. Even if the person does not know this language it is claimed that he will be able to use it "by a kind of miracle of tongues."[16]

May concludes, "This survey has shown that speaking-in-tongues is widespread and very ancient. Indeed it is probable that as long as man has had divination, curing, sorcery, and propitiation of spirits he has had glossolalia."[17]

Peter Freuchen, who lived among the Eskimos of Greenland for years, relates a tongues experience which he witnessed in a pagan ceremony. At the height of the frenzied rites a man and woman jumped up and began to speak in a strange tongue. Freuchen says, "If there is such a thing as speaking in tongues I heard it then."[18]

Without making any attempt to explain these cases of so-called glossolalia, we may at least be sure that, for one reason or another, people in various places and at various times have had experiences similar to glossolalia as found among some Christians today. Attempted explanations must take into consideration such possibilities as ecstatic production, self-hypnosis, demonic origin and playacting. Whatever the explanation, it is clear that pagans as well as Christians have their glossolalic experiences.

[16]Henri A. Junod, *The Life of A South African Tribe*, p. 445, as cited by May, p. 84.
[17]May, p. 92.
[18]Peter Freuchen, *Arctic Adventure; My Life in the Frozen North*, p. 135, as cited by H. J. Stolee, *Speaking in Tongues*, pp. 85-87.

7

Possible Explanations

If the present-day phenomenon of glossolalia is not of divine origin, it remains that it must originate in one of three ways. It may be faked, it may be demonic or it may be psychological in origin. Although on occasion there may be fake glossolalia, it is certain that this is not true of most cases of tongues among Christians today. The ease with which the speaking is performed, the lyrical, poetic, almost artful quality of many of its utterances, and the known integrity of many persons who speak in tongues argue against a faked origin. That glossolalia may be the product of demonism is a possibility, although such an explanation cannot be applied to tongues in general. It seems therefore that the origin of most current glossolalia lies in the area of the psychological. Speaking in tongues, if this be true, is the result of psychological forces at work within the personality of the glossolalic. As to exactly what these psychological forces are, there have been a number of suggestions.

Ecstasy

One of the oldest and most common explanations describes glossolalia as the result of ecstasy. Cutten is definite in characterizing it in this manner.

Whatever may be predicated of the psychological conditions of speaking with tongues in the New Testament, it is evident that the experience since then may be classed as ecstasy or allied phenomena. In ecstasy there is a condition of emotional exaltation, in which the one who experiences it is more or less oblivious of the external world, and loses to some extent his self-consciousness and his power of rational thought and self-control.[1]

According to this theory speaking in tongues is the result of a highly emotional state which lifts a person out of his ordinary frame of mind and causes him to pour out "impassioned utterances."

However, this view does not explain all cases of glossolalia, especially those found among some of the more moderate Pentecostals and the neo-Pentecostals, both of which testify that when they speak in tongues there is no unusually strong emotional pressure present. Emotions no doubt are aroused, but not to the extent that the condition may be called one of "emotional exaltation."

Hypnosis

Another explanation which has been suggested is hypnosis or autohypnosis. In the former a person directs his undivided attention toward some particular object usually bright in nature. He then lets his mind become blank and yields to the hypnotist's suggestions. If the hypnosis is effective the subject falls into a kind of sleep in which he is in a state of complete rapport with the hypnotist and performs the acts suggested by the latter.

[1]George B. Cutten, *Speaking with Tongues Historically and Psychologically Considered*, p. 157.

Although there are certain similarities between the glossolalic and the hypnotic states, it is not possible for hypnosis to explain adequately the phenomenon of speaking in tongues. For instance, there are numerous persons whose first experience of glossolalia came in private with nobody present to act as hypnotist. Furthermore, it is a known fact that the experience may be a recurring one which may be initiated or halted at will.

For this reason some have claimed tongues to be the product of autohypnosis or autosuggestion. In this case the suggestion comes from oneself rather than from a second person who acts as hypnotist. This may seem to explain the experiences of glossolalia which begin in private. It may be possible that a person so fixes his attention on an experience such as glossolalia that he himself provides the strong power of suggestion otherwise provided by the hypnotist. The glossolalic yields himself completely to what he conceives the tongues experience to be. In his mind he is yielding to the Holy Spirit so that the Spirit can speak through him. Because he knows what present-day tongues-speech is like, he breaks forth in the same kind of utterance. The experience may only come after days and nights of prayer and seeking which magnify the original suggestion until it produces a kind of self-hypnosis resulting in glossolalia.

Psychic Catharsis

Ira Jay Martin has explained tongues as a "psychic catharsis."[2] According to this view, a person seeks for maturity and self-fulfillment and fails to find it in any of the natural avenues of life. The result is frustration

[2]Ira Jay Martin, *Glossolalia in the Apostolic Church*, pp. 50-52, 54-55, 61, 100.

and conflict. When the light finally dawns and he sees that true personal maturity comes by faith and that righteousness is the product of forgiveness, the result is a sense of release and cleansing or catharsis. In many people this release produces a deep feeling of inner joy which is expressed in singing and testimony. In others whose temperament is of a different nature the result is spontaneous joy which can neither be contained nor expressed. The result is ecstatic utterance or glossolalia. This type of tongues, Martin calls "genuine," but later repetitions by the same individual which come frequently and almost at will are classified as "synthetic" and viewed as having a self-hypnotic character.[3] The person has become so taken up with tongues, the external by-product of his conversion, that this becomes an end in itself which he is able to reproduce at will. Martin says that "genuine" glossolalia may reoccur in the same person unexpectedly until his personality has been fully integrated and adjusted.

This explanation is a combination of a naturalistic and psychological understanding of conversion with the autohypnosis view described previously. Conversion is nothing more than a personality readjustment which in some persons produces tongues. Although such an explanation may seem to fit the account of the conversion of Cornelius in that tongues followed immediately on his acceptance of Peter's message, it fails to take into consideration many cases of tongues. Martin's view does not explain why most persons begin to speak in tongues at some time subsequent to their conversion as is almost always the case in current glossolalia. Both Pentecostals and neo-Pentecostals view tongues as an experience which invariably comes, not

[3] *Ibid.*, pp. 53-54.

at conversion but at a later time. Furthermore, the naturalistic explanation of conversion which is an integral part of the psychic catharsis theory renders the view contradictory to Scripture and therefore unacceptable.

Breakthrough of the Unconscious

Morton T. Kelsey and others have advanced the idea that glossolalia is to be explained in terms of the psychology of Carl G. Jung.[4] The latter has insisted that for sound mental health each person must make connection between the conscious and the unconscious spheres of his person. The unconscious level of being is viewed as a great underlying collection of human experience drawn from the human race as a whole. It is said that it is out of this "collective unconscious" that glossolalia arises. Kelsey explains:

> If the Jungian idea of the collective unconscious is accepted, speaking in tongues makes real sense, as a breakthrough into consciousness of a deep level of the collective unconscious similar to the dream. Linguistic patterns belonging to the past, to some other part of the present, or to some other level of being take possession of the individual and are expressed by him.[5]

This view takes us into areas where there is little possibility of objective, test-tube type of verification. It must therefore remain in the category of theory, being recognized as a possible explanation of the present-day phenomenon of glossolalia.

[4]Morton T. Kelsey, *Tongue Speaking: An Experiment in Spiritual Experience;* L. M. V. E. Vivier, *"Glossolalia"* (unpublished Doctor's dissertation).
[5]Kelsey, pp. 216-17.

Escape from Conflict

Another explanation arising in response to the tongues revival of the 60's is that suggested by James N. Lapsley and John H. Simpson,[6] who view glossolalia as an escape from conflict similar to such other motor mechanisms as automatic writing.[7] These authors suggest that the conflict may be between a primitive love for one's parent on the one hand and a hatred for and fear of the parent on the other hand. The tongues experience, then, is the ability to regress to the point where the person can voice his feelings without any conflict between love and hatred.[8] This means that the glossolalic has been able to return psychologically to that infantile stage prior to the beginning of the conflict of love and hatred toward the parent. The return is evidenced by what Lapsley and Simpson call "infantile babble," the vocal sounds expressed by the infant before the love-hate conflict arose.

According to this view the tongues-speaker is one who has a sense of inner conflict which is above average in intensity. It is denied that most glossolalics are to be considered as mentally ill, but rather it is suggested that the conflict producing glossolalia is similar to that which results in mental illness. In fact, glossolalia, by reducing such conflict, may be a preventative of mental illness.[9] This is in keeping with findings which tend to show that persons who speak in tongues are people who come from problem homes and who find life filled with

[6]James N. Lapsley and John H. Simpson, "Speaking in Tongues: Infantile Babble or Song of the Self?" *Pastoral Psychology*, XV (Sept., 1964), 16-24.

[7]*Ibid.*, p. 18.

[8]*Ibid.*, p. 19.

[9]*Ibid.*, pp. 20-21.

tension and conflict almost beyond their ability to bear.[10]

Exalted Memory

In view of the claims made by some that on occasion glossolalia has actually taken the form of a foreign language, mention should be made of one more possible explanation. Cutten has suggested, and cited authentic examples for, the occurrence of exalted memory.[11] In such cases a person retains in his memory utterances in a foreign language which cannot be recalled under normal circumstances. However, when the necessary psychological conditions have been met, the foreign expressions are released and the person speaks fluently in the language previously heard. Two instances of this type of tongues-speaking are reported by Cutten. In one case an illiterate servant in a delirium spoke at length in Latin, Hebrew and Greek. Upon investigation it was learned that when she had served in the home of a clergyman she had heard him recite long passages in these languages.[12]

Much of what a person hears is recorded more or less permanently in his mind. He may not be able at will to recall some of the facts stored there, but the information is there nevertheless. All that is needed is the right kind of stimulation to bring the stored facts to the surface of consciousness. And it is possible that such stimulation may be provided by one or more of the psychological factors which have been previously described in this section. For example, if glossolalia is the expres-

[10]*Ibid.*, pp. 16-17. Cf. Vivier; also William W. Wood, *Culture and Personality Aspects of the Pentecostal Holiness Religion*, pp. 97-110.
[11]Cutten, pp. 176 ff.
[12]*Ibid.*, p. 176.

sion of the collective unconscious as Kelsey believes, it may include the repetition of foreign expressions stored in the unconscious. Or if, as Lapsley and Simpson suggest, tongues are the result of regression with a view to conflict reduction, such regression may take one back to the time when the foreign language was heard and the stimulation of the experience may heighten the powers of recall with the result that the foreign expressions are reproduced.

Here, again, we can only assess this view as being a possibility inasmuch as its factors lie in areas where no positive verification can be produced. Along with the other views surveyed, however, it does serve to indicate kinds of possible explanations. Explanations such as these demonstrate that, if it is true that God withdrew the New Testament gift of tongues at the end of the apostolic age, it is possible that a somewhat similar phenomenon may be psychologically produced today. In the attempt to understand current glossolalia we are by no means confined to the view that it must be of divine origin.

A Suggested Solution

It is difficult to pin down the exact cause of current glossolalia for at least two reasons. First, the phenomenon is by its very nature subjective and not capable of verifiable examination. Second, there may well be different causes for different cases of tongues-speaking. However, although we may not be able to isolate one specific cause for the experience, we can suggest the general area in which the explanation is to be found. There is reason to believe that present-day glossolalia is an abnormal psychological occurrence. Specific items in the explanation of the phenomenon may vary from case to case, but the general explanation is the same for all instances.

The glossolalic first of all is apt to be a person who is so constructed psychologically that he is susceptible to the tongues experience. As a result of heredity and of environmental conditioning it is possible for him to speak in tongues, whereas for someone else it may be difficult or impossible. In many instances this psychological preparation seems to be provided in part by problem home situations, which produce a marked feeling of insecurity as well as difficulty in maintaining satisfying interpersonal relationships. For such a person life is filled with problems, tensions and conflicts.

It is only right that a person with this kind of problem should seek spiritual help from Christ and the church. The principles of Scripture, when properly understood and applied, are capable of alleviating such difficulties and providing the longed-for sense of security and acceptance. Some persons, however, when they learn of the glossolalic experience seek *in it* the solution to the problem. They read the New Testament accounts of the first century gift and hear the testimonies of the twentieth century experience, and the result is a growing desire to receive the gift.

Certainly one of the basic elements present in almost all cases of the initial experience of tongues is intense desire on the part of the candidate. It is often stated as the desire to receive all that God has for us. If God is waiting to give it, surely we should eagerly yearn for it. The desire is also fostered by the fact that the experience is supposedly miraculous. For many people it is natural to want to experience supernatural power and to witness its manifestation in such tangible ways as glossolalia. Furthermore, Christians are taught that they may and should experience the power of God (Eph. 1:18-23). The desire is also augmented by the group situation in which tongues usually are propagated. The gift is held up as the acme of Christian experience. To receive it is to gain the hallmark of spiritual prestige resulting in the feeling of group acceptance and divine approval. With such advantages in view, it is no wonder that persons, especially those with problem backgrounds, should intensely long for the gift.

Combined with the element of intense desire may be the factor of suggestion or a kind of autohypnosis. This is not to say that the full explanation of present-day glossolalia lies in the area of the hypnotic, but only that there may be hypnotic elements present in the tongues experience. In the glossolalic group the leader and others who speak in tongues provide something of the kind of suggestion which is present in hypnosis. To this should be added the suggestion—which can be exceedingly powerful for the Christian—provided by the New Testament accounts of tongues-speaking. Gradually these suggestive factors may work on the mind of the person considering tongues until the hypnotic influence takes effect and glossolalia results.

It is probable that there is a physiological as well as a psychological aspect to the explanation of glossolalia. The brain has been compared to a computer which is capable of storing facts to be recalled when demanded by the program fed into it.[13] Unlike the machine, however, the brain can store an almost unlimited number of facts. Everything that has ever entered the brain is

[13]Warren S. McCullough, "The Brain as a Computing Machine," *Electrical Engineering* (June, 1949), as cited by Stuart Bergsma, *Speaking with Tongues,* p. 11.

stored there waiting to be called forth when the proper stimulation occurs.

Normally what is drawn from the brain's reservoir of remembered facts is put together in logical order and used in rational thought processes which may be expressed in speaking and writing. However, there are exceptions. When a person dreams, images stored in the brain come to the surface of consciousness and are combined in arrangements that often are ludicrous. The reason seems to be that a shortcut process occurs wherein rationality does not control the manner in which the images are combined.

Just such a process seems to occur in glossolalia. Bergsma, a psychiatrist, suggests:

> The speaker takes the shortcut of a reflex action, bringing a dissociation upon himself, by which words do not go before the rational cerebral cortex for inspection, reflection and judgment as to whether they make sense, but are sent out directly via the efferent nerves as speech.[14]

As a result the speaker is released from adult inhibitions and controls of the speech pattern so that he freely combines sounds in new patterns. Included may be nonsense syllables, perhaps some foreign terms embedded in the subconscious, perhaps even longer passages of foreign speech previously heard and stored in the memory, and sometimes English words.

The result is usually a sense of release from tension and a feeling of joy. The release, no doubt, is partially psychologically grounded and may be explained by something like Lapsley and Simpson's conflict-reduction theory.[15] There is also the factor of divine ap-

[14]Bergsma, p. 16.
[15]Lapsley and Simpson, pp. 18-19.

proval which must be taken into consideration. Joy and peace come because the glossolalic feels that the gift of tongues is an evidence of God's acceptance and favor, the hallmark of spiritual attainment.

In reality, if the explanation suggested above is reasonably consonant with the facts, the experience of glossolalia is one of temporary abnormality. The brain is not functioning according to its normal pattern. A kind of short circuit has been produced and the rational area has been temporarily blocked out of the mental network. Although it would be inaccurate to say that such an occurrence is a form of mental illness, yet certain temporary similarities are apparent.

8

An Evaluation

Many people today testify to the blessing which speaking in tongues has brought to their lives, and the sincerity of their testimony is not to be doubted. They value the experience second only to their conversion. Certainly there are benefits to be received from the practice of glossolalia, even though the current phenomenon may not be the same as that which appeared in New Testament times. Therefore, before we examine the dangers inherent in present-day glossolalia, it is only right that we should survey its values.

Values of Glossolalia

Renewed Devotion

Many who have begun to speak in tongues witness to a new love for the Lord. Whereas before they were run-of-mill Christians, after the experience they are enthusiastic in their commitment to Him. Hearts once lukewarm are filled with a fervent desire to let Christ have His way.

Renewed Prayer Life

The tongues experience brings a new desire to pray and a new ease in praying with the result that more time is spent in prayer. The testimony of one who had recently received the gift of tongues was that, whereas it had previously been drudgery to pray for ten minutes, after tongues he could pray for two hours with ease.

Stress on Knowing God Experientially

Accompanying the tongues experience is an emphasis on a personal relationship with the Lord. This, of course, is the essence of any genuine Christian experience. However, Christianity for many has degenerated into a theoretical knowledge *about* God rather than being a personal knowledge *of* God. Speaking with tongues is viewed as a means of somehow speaking to God, "uttering the unutterable," expressing the feelings of the deepest level of one's soul which logical thought and speech cannot express. This is felt to be communion with God in the most personal sense. It is looked upon as the most intimate I-Thou relationship.

Renewed Emphasis of the Person of the Holy Spirit

In some ways the Holy Spirit has become the forgotten Person of the Trinity. Lip service is paid to His existence in creeds and in doctrinal statements, but the actual experience of the Spirit as a Person is for many completely unknown. But for those who have begun to speak in tongues the Spirit has ceased to be a doctrine and has become a Person. As is often true in cases of renewal, the pendulum has swung to the opposite extreme, often resulting in a certain undue emphasis on the Spirit. Nevertheless, for many a deficiency has been filled. The Holy Spirit has been brought back from oblivion and given a prominent place in Christian experience.

Emotion Returned to the Christian Life

The old-line denominations in far too many instances had crowded out of the churches anything which seemed to border on the emotional. Form replaced feeling, and creed supplanted experience. The result was that one major area of existence was omitted from the spiritual life of the church. Emotional needs were not being satisfied. Glossolalia has served to fill the void, for speaking with tongues is invariably an emotional experience. It results—so testify its adherents—in a sense of joy, peace and well-being which is entirely new. Love for God and for fellow Christians fills the heart, and the Christian experience once more becomes meaningful and satisfying.

Conflicts and Tensions Reduced

From a purely psychological point of view, glossolalia appears to have value. As Lapsley and Simpson point out, the experience serves, at least temporarily, to alleviate inner conflict and tension.[1] Whether or not their explanation of the process by which conflict is reduced is accepted, it is apparent that glossolalia does have value in this area. And as a result of the control of inner conflict, the glossolalic may find that his external relationships also are more satisfying and productive.

In at least these six ways it is apparent that the tongues experience is of value. It fills vacancies and satisfies needs. Consequently many Christians are enthusiastic propagators of the "full gospel," seeking to win their friends and associates to their viewpoint and to help them find a similar experience. Because He is

[1]James N. Lapsley and John H. Simpson, "Speaking in Tongues: Infantile Babble or Song of the Self?" *Pastoral Psychology,* XV (Sept., 1964), pp. 18-19.

working with imperfect human instruments, God sometimes uses erroneous understanding to bring blessing
into a life. Devotion to Christ may, on occasion, be
stimulated by Scripture misinterpreted and misapplied.

Although it is possible to cite certain benefits which
may be derived from the practice of glossolalia, it must
be recognized that none of these benefits is the product
of tongues as such. All can and should be experienced
apart from tongues. Furthermore, the dangers involved
in present-day glossolalia far outweigh the values which
may be forthcoming, and it is to these dangers that we
now address our attention.

Dangers of Glossolalia

A Psychological Substitute for the Supernatural

Present-day glossolalia is deceptive. It often is a
psychological attempt to recreate the supernatural gift
of the first century. Because of the complexity of human nature, when the proper conditions are present,
man is able to work himself into an experience which
he thinks to be the same as New Testament glossolalia.
Careful examination, however, has shown us how different such experiences seem to be from the phenomenon
clearly described in Acts 2. This is not to impugn the
sincerity of our tongues-speaking brethren. It is simply
to insist that in their sincerity they have often allowed
themselves to be deceived by a counterfeit experience
which does not measure up to the biblical standard.

Experience, the Criterion of Truth

It will be noted that the values listed above are all
experience centered. Although this does not detract
from their importance, it does reveal a significant characteristic of the phenomenon. Experience is all-im-

portant; unintentionally it is allowed to crowd even the
teaching of Scripture into second place. Truth to many
tongues speakers is determined, not so much by the
written Word of God as by personal experience. G.
Travers Sloyer rightly declares, "The lust after Christian experience has become a tidal wave in certain
quarters of the Church. To get an experience with God,
whether it is Scriptural or not, is the goal of even edu-
cated ministers."[2] Experience, as significant as it may
be, can never in itself be the criterion for truth. The
devil is a past master at manufacturing deceptive experiences. The only trustworthy standard is the Word
of God. Knowledge and understanding must, therefore,
never be sacrificed on the altar of experience. Just as
we dare not depend on feelings as a basis for assurance
of salvation, so we must not allow feelings and experience to supplant the Scriptures in the matter of tongues.

A Phenomenon Bordering on the Psychopathic

Let it be clearly understood that the author is not
suggesting in any way that the glossolalic is mentally
ill. We would not even want to say that he is necessarily slightly neurotic. But, if the previously suggested explanation of present-day tongues is reasonably
accurate, the glossolalic experience in such instances is
abnormal. It is a form of dissociation within the men-
tality of a person. It is in reality a separation which
blocks off the rational function of the brain with the
result that action is produced apart from rational control. Temporarily the tongues-speaker has entered a
pathological condition which is a perversion of the God-
intended function of the brain. It is toying with this
delicate precision instrument with which God has gifted

[2]G. Travers Sloyer, *Is This Revival?* p. 11.

us. It is transforming the seat of rationality into an irrational machine. In so doing a person contravenes God's purpose for man as a rational being.

An Escape Mechanism

Glossolalia is said to be a means of conflict reduction, an agent of integration within the personality resulting in the sense of joy, peace and well-being which follows the experience. However, whatever there is of conflict reduction in glossolalia, it is not a cure since it deals only with the symptoms and not with the real causes of a man's tensions. Like all escape mechanisms, its relief is temporary rather than thoroughgoing and permanent. It covers up rather than eradicates the problems which often provide the fertile ground from which tongues spring.

An Encouragement to Spiritual Pride

Any spiritual accomplishment may be an occasion for spiritual pride; and the loftier the attainment, the greater the temptation to haughtiness. This seems to be singularly true of tongues. Often viewed as the apex of spiritual experience, when it has been attained glossolalia is easily productive of self-exaltation. The glossolalics tend to gravitate together and to form spiritual cliques, the members of which, because of the very nature of the case, cannot help but feel superior. And, let it be remembered, no pride is quite as inconsistent or quite as vicious as "pride of grace."

Substitution of Sight for Faith

Faith is not easy, whether to attain or to retain. Clothed as we are in flesh, Christians constantly are tempted to seek the things which are seen instead of the

things not seen. We want to see the tangible evidence
of God's presence rather than to take it by faith. This
lingering characteristic of spiritual childhood comprises
one of the dangers of speaking with tongues. The supposed miracle is something apparent to the senses, a tangible activity of God which demands little more faith
than it takes to know that the wind is blowing when we
hear it. Faith, however, knows that God is present, that
He is active in the affairs of men, although He cannot
be seen with the eye of flesh or heard with the physical
ear. But the desire for the glossolalic experience moves
on a lower level, substituting sight for faith.

Shortcut to Spiritual Attainment

Spiritual accomplishment is not easy to come by. It
is the result of agonizing growth, of defeat after defeat
followed by victory, of wrestling in prayer and searching the Word of God. Christian character is forged by
blow after blow on the anvil of daily experience. It
never comes quickly, but, like maturity of any kind, it
is the product of the slow process of growth. How shal-
low, then, is the view of many glossolalics who assume
that spiritual maturity has suddenly arrived in one
short hour of ecstatic experience. This is not exag-
gerating, for such has been the testimony of some, and
such is the apparent assumption of others who are not
quite as frank. Francis Geddes, director of the Religious
Research Foundation, says, "Those who speak in
tongues say you get spiritual maturity for nothing."[3]
Herein lies its deceptiveness—the promise of easy accomplishment when in reality such is impossible.
Tongues are no substitute for holiness of life; ecstasy

[3]Donovan Bess, " 'Speaking in Tongues': The High Church
Heresy," *The Nation*, CXCVII (Sept. 28, 1963), 176.

cannot take the place of uprightness and Christian integrity.

An Instrument of the Flesh

For some, glossolalia becomes something like a spiritual toy, something with which it is fun to play, something engaged in for the kick they get out of it. Granted, this is not true of all who speak in tongues. Nevertheless, such an attitude is altogether too prevalent. One leader of a tongues group is quoted by Lapsley and Simpson as saying, "Is there anything which is more fun than praising God?"[4] The context in which this question was asked made it plain that the speaker was referring to glossolalia. When tongues are practiced for the fun one can get out of the experience they are catering to the flesh. They become comparable to alcohol or a drug in that they produce a temporary type of intoxication which is gratifying to the flesh. Obviously, to prostitute what is supposed to be a spiritual experience for the satisfaction of the carnal nature is a tragic exchange.

A Divisive Factor

Experience has demonstrated that glossolalia tends to create division in the church. Those who have it often tend to feel superior to those who don't. Still more divisive is the evangelistic fervor with which tongues people attempt to make converts of nonglossolalic Christians. This has often resulted in Pentecostal churches proselyting members from non-Pentecostal churches. It has produced purposeful penetration

[4]Lapsley and Simpson, "Speaking in Tongues: Token of Group Acceptance and Divine Approval," *Pastoral Psychology,* XV (May, 1964), 54.

of non-Pentecostal churches by tongues people. The author once heard a well-known Pentecostal evangelist and healer explicitly urge people from fundamental churches to go back and stir up trouble on the excuse that those churches were cold and dead and needed to be stirred up. Often small extrachurch Bible study groups are formed to propagate tongues with the result that a schismatic wedge is introduced into the church. It is common for glossolalics to feel that they are under divine compulsion to spread the tongues message and to make as many converts as they can. The New Testament nowhere even hints that any attempt should be made to convert people to tongues. The only evangelism the New Testament knows is that which seeks to win the lost to Christ.

A Possible Tool of Satan

The fact that glossolalia has been known among pagans as part of their religious practices suggests the possibility that in some instances even among Christians tongues may be demon-inspired. The requirement that one must yield oneself completely in order to experience tongues opens one to possible entrance and control by demonic powers. The surrender of the rational faculty of discrimination and of understanding which tongues make necessary is a dangerous surrender that Satan may well use without the Christian realizing it. We must never give up the rational power to "try the spirits whether they are of God" (I John 4:1).

Tongues—to speak or not to speak? That is the question which we have sought to answer. If God were once again to give the supernatural New Testament gift, the answer would unquestionably be in the affirmative. However, since the evidence indicates that God is not so acting today, the response must be a refusal to become involved. Values there may well be in the experience, but the dangers which are present far outweigh the values. Therefore wisdom counsels that we not seek an easy shortcut to spiritual maturity. Instead let us employ the normal means to develop the love and devotion, the vital prayer life and the intimate awareness of God's presence which mark the mature Christian life.

Bibliography

Arndt, W. F., and Gingrich, F. W. *A Greek-English Lexicon of the New Testament.* Chicago: U. Chicago, 1957.

Augustine. "Homilies on the First Epistle of John."

Beare, Frank W. "Speaking with Tongues," *Journal of Biblical Literature,* LXXXIII (Sept., 1964), 228-46.

Bellshaw, William G. "Confusion of Tongues," *Bibliotheca Sacra,* CXX (Apr.-June, 1963), 145-53.

Bergsma, Stuart. *Speaking with Tongues.* Grand Rapids: Baker, 1965.

Bess, Donovan. " 'Speaking in Tongues': The High Church Heresy," *The Nation,* CXCVII (Sept. 28, 1963), 173-77.

Brumback, Carl. *Suddenly . . . from Heaven: A History of the Assemblies of God.* Springfield, Mo.: Gospel Pub., 1961.

———. *"What Meaneth This?" A Pentecostal Answer to a Pentecostal Question.* Springfield, Mo.: Gospel Pub., 1947.

Chrysostom. "Homilies on the First Epistle of Paul the Apostle to the Corinthians."

Currie, S. D. "Speaking in Tongues; Early Evidence Outside the New Testament Bearing on Glossais," *Interpretation,* XIX (July, 1965), 274-94.

Cutten, George B. *Speaking with Tongues Historically and Psychologically Considered.* New Haven: Yale U., 1927.

Drummond, A. L. *Edward Irving and His Circle, Including Some Considerations of the "Tongues" Movement in the Light of Modern Psychology.* London: J. Clark, 1937.

Farrell, Frank. "Outburst of Tongues: The New Penetration," *Christianity Today*, VII (Sept. 13, 1963), 1166-70.

Freuchen, Peter. *Arctic Adventure; My Life in the Frozen North*. New York: Farrar, 1935.

Frodsham, Stanley H. *With Signs Following: The Story of the Pentecostal Revival in the Twentieth Century*. Springfield, Mo.: Gospel Pub., 1941.

Gee, Donald. *Concerning Spiritual Gifts*. Springfield, Mo.: Gospel Pub., n.d.

Graham, D. C. *Religion in Szechwan Province, China*, Smithsonian Miscellaneous Collections, LXXX, 4. Washington: Smithsonian Inst., 1928.

Gromacki, Robert G. *The Modern Tongues Movement*. Philadelphia: Presb. & Ref., 1967.

Hayes, D. A. *The Gift of Tongues*. Cincinnati: Jennings & Graham, 1913.

Hills, James W. L. "The New Pentecostalism: Its Pioneers and Promoters," *Eternity*, XIV (July, 1963), 17-18.

Hitt, Russell. "The New Pentecostalism: An Appraisal," *Eternity*, XIV (July, 1963), 10-16.

Hoekema, Anthony. *What About Tongues Speaking?* Grand Rapids: Eerdmans, 1966.

Horn, W. M. "Speaking in Tongues; a Retrospective Appraisal," *Lutheran Quarterly*, XVII (Nov., 1965), 316-29.

Irenaeus. "Against Heresies."

Jennings, George J. "An Ethnological Study of Glossolalia," *Journal of the American Scientific Affiliation*, XX (Mar., 1968), 5-16.

Johnson, S. Lewis. "The Gift of Tongues and the Book of Acts," *Bibliotheca Sacra*, CXX (Oct.-Dec., 1963), 311.

Junod, Henri A. *The Life of a South African Tribe*. Neuchâtel, Switzerland: Imprimerie Attinger Frères, 1913.

Kaasa, Harris. "An Historical Evaluation" in "A Symposium on Speaking in Tongues," *Dialog*. Vol. II (Spring, 1963).

Keiper, Ralph L. *Tongues and the Holy Spirit*. Chicago: Moody, 1963.

Kelsey, Morton T. *Tongue Speaking: An Experiment in Spiritual Experience.* Garden City, N. Y.: Doubleday, 1964.

Langston, Edward. "What Are Demons?" *The London Quarterly and Holborn Review* (Jan., 1954), p. 30.

Lapsley, James N., and Simpson, John H. "Speaking in Tongues: Token of Group Acceptance and Divine Approval," *Pastoral Psychology,* XV (May, 1964), 48-55.

————. "Speaking in Tongues: Infantile Babble or Song of the Self?" *Pastoral Psychology,* XV (Sept., 1964), 16-24.

Latourette, Kenneth S. *A History of Christianity.* New York: Harper, 1953.

Lovekin, Arthur A. "Glossolalia: A Critical Study of Alleged Origins, the New Testament and the Early Church." Unpublished Master's thesis, Graduate School of Theology, U. of the South, Sewanee, Tenn., 1962.

McCullough, Warren S. "The Brain as a Computing Machine," *Electrical Engineering* (June, 1949).

MacDonald, William G. "Glossolalia in the New Testament," *Bulletin of the Evangelical Theological Society,* VII (Spring, 1964), 59-68.

Mackie, Alexander. *The Gift of Tongues, A Study in Pathologic Aspects of Christianity.* New York: Doran, 1921.

Martin, Ira Jay. *Glossolalia in the Apostolic Church.* Berea, Ky.: Berea College, 1960.

May, L. Carlyle. "A Survey of Glossolalia and Related Phenomena in Non-Christian Religions," *American Anthropologist,* LVIII (Feb., 1956), 75-96.

Oman, John B. "On 'Speaking in Tongues': A Psychological Analysis," *Pastoral Psychology,* XIV (Dec., 1963), 48-51.

Phillips, McCandlish. "And There Appeared to Them Tongues of Fire," *The Saturday Evening Post,* CCXXXVII (May 16, 1964), 31-40.

Pike, James A. "Pastoral Letter Regarding 'Speaking in Tongues,'" *Pastoral Psychology,* XV (May, 1964), 56-61.

Rice, Robert. "Charismatic Revival," *Christian Life,* XXV (Nov., 1963), 30-32.

Rogers, L. "Gift of Tongues in the Post-Apostolic Church, A.D. 100-400," *Bibliotheca Sacra,* CXXII (Apr.-June, 1965), 134-43.

Samarin, William J. "The Linguisticality of Glossolalia," *Hartford Quarterly,* VIII (Summer, 1968), 49-75.

Sherrill, John L. *They Speak with Other Tongues.* Westwood, N. J.: Revell, 1965.

Shumway, C. W. "A Critical History of Glossolalia." Unpublished Doctor's dissertation, Boston U., 1919.

Sloyer, G. Travers. *Is This Revival?* Schenectady: Peniel Tracts, 1964.

Stagg, Frank; Hinson, E. Glenn; and Oates, Wayne E. *Glossolalia, Tongue Speaking in Biblical, Historical and Psychological Perspective.* Nashville: Abingdon, 1967.

Stahlin, Gustav. *"Isos, isotēs, isotimos," Theological Dictionary of the New Testament.* Ed. Gerhard Kittel, trans. G. W. Bromiley. Grand Rapids: Eerdmans, 1965.

Stolee, H. J. *Speaking in Tongues.* Minneapolis: Augsburg, 1963.

"Symposium on Speaking in Tongues," *Dialog,* II (Spring, 1963), 152-59.

"Symposium on the Tongues Movement," *Bibliotheca Sacra,* CXX (July-Sept., 1963), 224-33; (Oct.-Dec., 1963), 309-21.

Tertullian. "Against Marcion."

Van Elderen, Bastian. "Glossolalia in the New Testament," *Bulletin of the Evangelical Theological Society,* VII (Spring, 1964), 53-58.

Vivier, L. M. V. E. "Glossolalia." Unpublished Doctor's dissertation, U. Witwatersrand, Johannesburg, 1960.

Walker, Dawson. *The Gift of Tongues.* Edinburgh: T. & T. Clark, 1906.

Welmers, William E. Letter to *Christianity Today,* VIII (Nov. 8, 1963), 127-28.

Wolfram, Walter A. "The Sociolinguistics of Glossolalia." Unpublished Master's thesis, Hartford Sem. Found., Hartford, Conn., 1966.

Wood, William W. *Culture and Personality Aspects of the Pentecostal Holiness Religion.* The Hague: Mouton, 1965.